He Dwells in Your Soul

Bede Jarrett, O.P.

He Dwells in Your Soul

Encountering the Living God Within You

SOPHIA INSTITUTE PRESS®
Manchester, New Hampshire

He Dwells in Your Soul: Encountering the Living God Within You was originally published in New York in 1918 by the Cathedral Library Association under the title *The Abiding Presence of the Holy Ghost in the Soul*. This 1998 edition by Sophia Institute Press contains slight revisions throughout the text.

Sophia Institute Press®

Box 5284, Manchester, NH 03108

1-800-888-9344

Nihil obstat: Arthur J. Scanlan, D.D., *Censor Deputatus*
Imprimatur: John Cardinal Farley, Archbishop of New York
March 21, 1918

Library of Congress Cataloging-in-Publication Data

Jarrett, Bede, 1881-1934.
    [Abiding presence of the Holy Ghost in the soul]
    He dwells in your soul : encountering the living God within
        you / Bede Jarrett.
        p.   cm.
    Originally published : The abiding presence of the Holy Ghost
        in the soul. New York : Cathedral Library Association, 1918.
    ISBN 0-918477-70-0 (pbk. : alk. paper)
    1. Holy Spirit. 2. Presence of God.   I. Title.
    BT121.2.J37 1998
    231.7 — dc21   98-10397 CIP

98 99 00 01 02 10 09 08 07 06 05 04 03 02 01

Contents

Our presence with God

God's gifts within us

Preface

Hardly anything can render us more sensible of our worth and Christian dignity than does the teaching of our Lord on the indwelling of the Spirit of God. The wonderful beauty of this teaching, while it deepens our acquaintance with His mysterious governance of the universe and reveals to us the hidden beauties of our soul's life, should bring also its measure of comfort, for whatever makes us conscious of the intimacy of God's dealing with us lessens life's greatest trouble, its loneliness.

Bede Jarrett, O.P.
Our Lady of Lourdes
New York
February 11, 1918

He Dwells in Your Soul

God's presence within us

God is present in all things

Scripture is very full of the idea of the nearness of God
to His creation; the Old Testament is alive with that
inspiration, for there is hardly a chapter or verse that
does not insist upon that truth. Naturally the New Testament, teaching so tenderly the Fatherhood of God, is
even more explicit and beautiful in its references to
this intimate relationship. To the Athenians, St. Paul
can develop no other point than this, and he finds in
moving accents an eloquent appeal voiced by the
touching dedication of an altar to the unknown God.[1]
Now, this notion of God's nearness to His world depends

[1] Acts 17:22-23. The biblical references in the following pages are based on the Douay-Rheims version of
the Old and New Testaments. Where applicable, quo-
tations have been cross-referenced with the differing
names and enumeration in the Revised Standard Version, using the following symbol: (RSV =).

for its full appreciation on the central doctrine of creation. He has made the world; in consequence it is impressed with His personality; the more vigorous the artificer—the more vigorous, that is, in character, will, and personality—the more is his work stamped with his individuality; hence, the tremendous personality of God must be traceable everywhere in the things He has made.

When we say God is everywhere, we mean that He is in all things because He made all things. Not only does the whole world lie outstretched before His eye and is governed by His power, but He Himself lurks at the heart of everything. By Him things have come into existence, and so wholly is that existence of theirs His gift, that were He to withdraw His support, they would sink back into nothingness.

It is a perpetual remark about man's works that they outlast him. Organizations we have toiled to establish outgrow our fostering care, perhaps grow tired of our interference and long to be free of our regulations. Wordsworth[2] tells how a monk in Spain, pointing to the pictures on the walls of the monastery, which remained

[2] William Wordsworth (1770-1850), English poet.

while the generations looking at them passed away, judged: "We are the shadows, they the substance." But the relationship established by creation is of a far greater dependence, so that nothing God has made can exist without His support. Out of human acts it is only music that bears some resemblance to this, for when the voice is silent, there is no longer any song.

God, then, is within all creation, because He is its cause. He is within every stone and leaf and child. Nothing, with life or without, evil or good, can fail to contain Him as the source of its energy, its power, and its existence; He is "the soul's soul." Not only, therefore, must I train myself to see with reverence that everything contains Him, but I must especially realize His intimacy and relationship to myself. Religion, indeed, in practice is little else than my personal expression of that relationship.

In my prayers, in my troubles, in my temptations, I have to turn to God, not without but within; not to someone above me or beneath me, supporting me, but right at the core of my being. I can trace up to its source every power of my soul—my intelligence, my will, my love, my anger, and my fear—and I shall find Him there. There is nothing that does not open its doors to Him as innermost in its shrine. Wholly is God everywhere, not as some immense being that with its hugeness fills the world, but as something that is within every creature He has made.

2

God's presence is greater in some things than in others

God is intimate with all creation because He made it, for creation implies that God remains within—supporting, upholding. God is within everything, and therefore He is everywhere. But while we thus believe that God is wholly everywhere, we also believe something which seems the exact opposite, for we believe that God is more in some places than in others, more in some people than in others.

How is it, if God is wholly everywhere, that He can be more here than there? To understand this we must also understand that every created thing shares somehow in God's being. He communicates Himself to it in some fashion, for apart from Him it could have no perfections. We have a way of saying that we reflect God's greatness and that we are "broken lights" of Him. But that is far short of the truth: we do more than reflect; we actually have some participation in God, so that St. Thomas boldly takes over a saying of Plato: "The individual nature of a thing consists in the way it participates in the perfections of God."[3] Not, of course, that there is any community of being, but rather a direct participation.

Now, since everything participates in God and since some things are more excellent than others, it stands to reason that some things express God better than others. The eyes of a dog often are pitiful to see, because we can note its evident desire and yet its impossibility to express its feelings. To seeing minds the whole of nature has the same pitifulness. It is always endeavoring to express God, the inexpressible.

Yet the higher a thing is in the scale of being, the more of God it expresses, for it participates more in God's being. The more life a thing has and the more freedom it acquires, the nearer does it approach God and the more divinity it holds. Man, by his intelligence,

---

[3] St. Thomas Aquinas (Dominican philosopher, theologian, and Doctor of the Church; c. 1225-1274), *Summa Theologica*, I, Q. 14, art. 6.

his deeper and richer life, and his finer freedom, stands at the head of visible creation and, in consequence, is more fully a shrine of God than are lower forms of life. He bears a closer resemblance to the divine intelligence and will and has a greater share in them. It is, then, in that sense that we arrange in ascending order inanimate creation, the vegetable kingdom, the animal kingdom, and man.

Consequently we can now see in what sense God is said to be more in one thing than in another. He is more in it because He exercises Himself more in one thing than in another; one thing expresses more than another the perfections of God because it shares more deeply than another that inner being of God. The more nearly anything or anyone is united to God, the more does His power exercise itself in them. Since God's gifts are variously distributed and are of various degrees, we are justified in saying that although He is wholly everywhere, He may be more fully here than there; just as, although my soul is in every part of my being, it is more perfectly in the brain than elsewhere, because there it exercises itself more fully and with more evidence of expression. Thus we say God is more in a man's soul than anywhere else in creation, since in

He Dwells in Your Soul

a man's soul God is more perfectly expressed. It is therefore with great reverence that I should regard all creation, but with especial reverence that I should look to
the dignity of every human soul.

3

God dwells most fully
in the souls of the just

While God is in everything in creation, He dwells in the just by grace. Scripture quite noticeably uses the word *dwelling* when it wishes to express the particular way in which God is present in the souls of the just. He *is* in all things; but in the just He *dwells*. The same word actually is applied to the presence of God in the souls of those in grace, as is used when speaking of God's presence in the temple. But here again it is necessary to say that God's dwelling in the temple never implied He was not elsewhere, but did imply that somehow His presence in the temple was quite different from the way in which He was present elsewhere.

The same kind of difference between the presence of God in all created nature and His presence in the souls of the just is intended by the careful use in Scripture of the word *dwelling*, that is, that God has, over and above His ordinary presence in every single created thing, a further and especial presence in the hearts of those in friendship with Him by grace; and this new presence is a fuller and richer presence, whereby God's excellences and perfections are more openly displayed.

Another way in which the same idea is pressed home in the New Testament is by the word *sent*, or *given*. Frequently, in the last discourse of our Lord on the night before He suffered, He spoke to the Apostles of the Holy Spirit—the Paraclete, the Comforter—who was to be sent, or given.[4] Now, ordinarily, by using the expression "sending someone," we imply that now the person sent is where he was not before, that he has passed from here to there. Obviously our Lord cannot really mean that only after His Crucifixion and Ascension would the Holy Spirit be found in the hearts of the Apostles, for we have already insisted that the Holy Spirit must be at the heart of every creature, by virtue of its very creation. Hence the only possible meaning is that the Holy Spirit will descend upon the Apostles and become present within them in some new

[4] Cf. John 14:26.

fashion in which He was not before. "Because you are His children, God has sent into your hearts the Spirit of His Son, whereby you cry, 'Abba, Father.'"[5] From the beginning the Holy Spirit had been within them; now His presence there is new and productive of new effects.

By God's indwelling, then, effected by grace, the Holy Spirit now is present in the soul differently from the way in which He is present by creation. By creation He is wholly everywhere, yet more in the higher forms than in the lower, for He is able to express more of Himself in the higher. Among these highest forms of visible creation—namely, man—there are again degrees of His presence, so that even among men, He is more in one than in another. This gradation is in proportion to their grace. The more holy and sanctified they become, the more does the Holy Spirit dwell in them, the more fully is He sent, and the more completely is He given, whereas the Book of Wisdom says expressly that God does not dwell in sinners.[6]

As soon as I am in a state of grace, the Holy Spirit dwells in me in this new and wonderful way, takes up

[5] Cf. Gal. 4:6.
[6] Cf. Wisd. 1:4.

He Dwells in Your Soul

His presence in me in this new fashion. It is precisely, then, by our faith and hope and love that this is effected, so that the individual soul under God's own movement does help to bring about this union of God and man. In all the rest of creation, God is present by His action; in the souls of the just, it is true to say that He is present by theirs.

4

How God is present in our souls

We have taken it for granted that God, then, is present somehow in the soul by grace. We have now to consider what sort of a presence this really is. Do we mean absolutely that God the Holy Spirit is truly in the soul Himself, or do we, by some metaphor or vague expression, mean that He is merely exerting Himself there in some new and special way? Perhaps it is only that, by means of the sevenfold gifts,[7] He has a tighter hold on us and can bring us more completely under the sweet dominion of His will.

All that is true, but it is not enough, for we do absolutely mean what we say when we declare that, by grace, the Holy Spirit of God is present within the

[7] The seven gifts of the Holy Spirit are knowledge, wisdom, understanding, counsel, fortitude, piety, and fear of the Lord (Cf. Isa. 11:2).

soul. Scripture is exceedingly full of the truth of this and is always insisting on this presence of the Holy Spirit. St. Paul, especially, notes it over and over again, and in his letter to the Romans repeats it in very forcible language: "But you are not in the flesh, but in the spirit, if it be that the Spirit of God dwells in you."[8] And he goes on in that same chapter to imply that this presence is a part of grace.

To some it will seem curious to find that the Fathers of the Church in earliest ages were not only convinced of the fact of this presence, but appealed triumphantly to it as accepted even by heretics. When, in the early days, a long controversy raged as to whether the Holy Spirit was really God or not, the Fathers argued that since this indwelling of the Spirit was acknowledged on all hands, and since it was proper to God only to dwell in the heart of man, the only possible conclusion was that the Holy Spirit was divine.

The value of the argument is not here in question, but it is interesting to find that this presence was so generally believed in as part of the Christian Faith. In the acts of the martyrs too, there are frequent references to

[8] Rom. 8:9.

this, as when St. Lucy[9] declared to the judge that the Spirit of God dwelt in her, and that her body was in very truth the temple and shrine of God. Again, Eusebius[10] relates in his *History* that Leonidas, the father of Origen,[11] used to kneel by the bedside of the sleeping boy and devoutly and reverently kiss his son's breast as the tabernacle wherein God dwelt. The child in his innocence and grace is indeed the fittest home on earth for God.

This presence, then, of God in the soul is a real, true presence, as real and true as the presence of Our Lord Himself in the Blessed Sacrament of the Eucharist. We look on all that mystery as very wonderful, and indeed it is, that day by day we can be made one with God the Son by receiving His body and blood; we know the value of visits to His hidden presence, the quiet and calm peace such visits produce in our souls; yet so long as we are in a state of grace, the same holds true of the Holy Spirit within us.

[9] Virgin who was martyred in the persecution by Diocletian (died 303).

[10] Bishop of Caesarea, known as the "Father of Church History" (c. 260-340).

[11] St. Leonidas (died 202), martyr during the persecution in Alexandria; Origen (c. 185-254), Alexandrian biblical critic, theologian, and spiritual writer.

He Dwells in Your Soul

We are not indeed made one with the Holy Spirit in a substantial union, such as united God with man in the sacred Incarnation; nor is there any overpowering of our personality so that it is swamped by a Divine Person, but we retain it absolutely. The simplest comparison is our union with our Lord in the Holy Eucharist, wherein we receive Him really and truly and are made partakers of His divinity. By grace, then, we receive, really and truly, God the Holy Spirit and are made partakers of His divinity. If, then, we genuflect to the tabernacle in which the Blessed Sacrament is reserved and treat our Communions as the most solemn moments of our day, then equally we must hold in reverence every simple soul in a state of grace—the souls of others and our own.

5

We can experience God's presence in our own souls

The fact, then, of this presence has been established and its nature explained. It is a real presence, a real union between the soul and God the Holy Spirit. We have, however, a further point to elucidate: the mode whereby this presence is effected. Now, this is twofold insofar as this presence of the Spirit affects the mind and heart of man.

First, then, we take the knowledge of God that is generated in the soul by this presence. From natural knowledge we can not only deduce the existence of God, but in some way also deduce His nature. Not only do we know from the world which He has made that He certainly must Himself have a true existence, but from it we can even, gradually and carefully, although certainly with some vagueness, discover God's own divine attributes. His intelligence is evident, as are His power, His wisdom, His beauty, His Providence, and His care for created nature. The pagans, merely from the world about them, painfully, and after many years and with much admixture of error, could yet in the end have their beautiful thoughts about God, and by some amazing instinct have stumbled upon truths which Christianity came fully to establish. The writings of Plato and Aristotle, of some Eastern teachers, and of some of the kings and priests of Egypt are evidence of the possibility of the natural knowledge about God.

Faith, then, came as something over and above the possibilities of nature, not merely as regards the contents, but also as regards the kind of knowledge it gives us. Reason deduces truths about God, and therefore attains God indirectly. It is like getting an application by letter from an unknown person and guessing his character from the handwriting, the paper, the ink, the spelling, and the style. Possibly by this means, a very fair estimate may be formed of his capacities and his fitness for the position which we desire him to fill. But faith implies a direct contact with the person who has written the letter. Before us is spread what Longfellow has called "the manuscript of God,"[12] and from it we deduce God's character. Then faith comes and puts us straight into connection with God Himself.

The "theological virtues" is the name given to faith, hope, and charity, because they all have God for their direct and proper object. Faith, then, attains to the very substance of God. It is indeed inadequate insofar as all human forms of thought can only falteringly represent God as compared with the fullness that shall be revealed hereafter; still, for all that, it gives us not indirect, but direct knowledge of Him. From seeing His handiwork, I do not deduce by faith what God is like, but I know what He is like from His descriptions of Himself.

Now, the indwelling of the Spirit of God gives us a knowledge of God even more wonderful than faith gives, for even faith has to be content with God's descriptions of Himself. In faith I am indeed listening to a Person who is telling me all about Himself. He is the very truth, and all He says is commended to me by the most solemn and certain of motives; but I am still very far from coming absolutely into direct and absolute

[12]Henry Wadsworth Longfellow (American poet; 1807-1882), "Fiftieth Birthday of Agassiz."

experience of God. That, indeed, fully and absolutely, can be achieved only in Heaven. It is only there, in the Beatific Vision, that the veils will be wholly torn aside and there will be a face-to-face sight of God, no longer by means of created, and therefore limited, ideas, but an absolute possession of God Himself.

Yet although I must wait for Heaven before I can achieve this absolutely, it is nonetheless true that I can begin it on earth by means of this indwelling of the Spirit of God. This real presence of God in my soul can secure for me what is called an experiential knowledge of God, such as undoubtedly I have. It is not only that I believe, but I know. Not only have I been told about God, but, at least in passing glimpses, I have seen Him. We may almost say to the Church what the men of Sichar said to the woman of Samaria: "We now believe, not for thy saying, for we ourselves have heard and know."[13] "For the Spirit Himself giveth testimony to our spirit that we are the sons of God."[14]

[13]John 4:42.
[14]Rom. 8:16.

6

We can love the Holy Spirit who dwells within us

There is something that unites us more closely to our friends than knowledge does, and this is love. Knowledge may teach us about them, may unlock for us gradually throughout life ever more wonderful secrets of their goodness and strength and loyalty. But knowledge of itself pushes us irresistibly on to something more. The more we know of that which is worth knowing, the more we must love it.

Now, love is greater than knowledge whenever knowledge itself does not really unite us to the object of our knowledge; so St. Paul can deliberately put charity above faith, since faith is the knowledge of God by means of ideas which are themselves created and limited and inadequate, while charity sweeps us up and carries us right along to God Himself. Hence it was an axiom among the medieval theologians that love is more unifying than knowledge, so that in the real indwelling of the Holy Spirit in our hearts, we must expect to find not only that He is the object of our intelligence, but also that He has a place in our hearts. Indeed, it is impossible to conceive any experiential knowledge which does not also include in it the notion of love.

This love or friendship between ourselves and the Holy Spirit—if by *friendship* we mean anything like that of which we have experience in our human relations—implies three things. First of all, friendship implies that we do not love people for what we can get out of them; that would be an insult to a friend, for it would mean selfishness or even animal passion. Friendship implies that we come for what we can give far more than that we come for what we can get. "We love because we have helped" is more often the true order of the origins of friendship than "we help because we have loved."

Secondly, friendship, to be complete, must be mutual. There may indeed be love when in this world some poor, forlorn soul is never requited in its affection, but that is not what we mean by *a friend* or by *friendship*. Friendship implies action, a fellow feeling, a desire for each other, a sympathy.

We can love the Holy Spirit

Thirdly, friendship also implies necessarily a common bond of likeness, or similarity of condition or life,
some equality. Of course, it is evident from classic in-
stances that friendship may exist between a shepherd
lad and the son of a king (although perhaps Jonathan's
princedom was very little removed from shepherd life),[15]
yet the very friendship itself must produce equality between them. Said the Latin proverb: "Friendship either
finds or makes men equal."

Now, therefore, to be perfectly literal in our use of
the word, we must expect to find these things reproduced in our friendship with the Spirit of God; and,
wonderful as it is, these things are reproduced. For God
certainly loves us for no benefit that He can obtain
from His love. He certainly had no need of us, nor do
we in any sense fill up anything that is wanting in His
life. Before we were, or the world was created, the Ever
Blessed Three-in-One enjoyed to the full the complete
peace and joy and energy of existence. We are no late
development of His being, but only came because of
His inherent goodness that was always prodigal of itself. He is our friend, not for His need, but for ours. He

[15]Cf. 1 Kings 18:1-3 (RSV = 1 Sam. 18:1-3).

27

is our friend, not for what He can get, but for what He can give — His life. Again, His friendship is certainly mutual, for as St. John tells: "Let us therefore love God because God first hath loved us."[16] There is no yearning on our part which is not more than paralleled on His. I can say not only that I love God, but that He is my friend.

Thirdly, I may even dare to assert that there is a common bond of likeness and equality between myself and Him. He has stooped to my level only that He may lift me to His own. He became man that He might make man God, and so, equally, the Holy Spirit dwells in me that I may dwell in Him. "Friendship either finds or makes men equal." It found us apart; it makes us one. He, divine and perfect, came to me, human and imperfect. By grace I am raised to a supernatural level. I know Him in some sort as He is; I am immediately united to Him by the bond of love.

[16] 1 John 4:19.

His presence within us
is a foretaste of Heaven

This union, then, between God and my soul, effected by grace, is real and true. It is something more than faith can secure; a nearer relationship; a deeper, more personal knowledge; a more ardent and personal love. Indeed, so wonderful is the union effected that the teaching of the Church has been forcibly expressed in Pope Leo XIII's encyclical,[17] by saying that the only difference between it and the Vision of Heaven is a difference of condition or state—a difference purely accidental, not essential. Heaven, with all its meaning, its wonders of which eye and ear and heart are ignorant,[18] can be begun here. Moreover, it must be insisted upon

[17]Pope Leo XIII (1810-1903), *On the Holy Ghost*.
[18]Cf. Isa. 64:4; 1 Cor. 2:9.

that this is not merely given to chosen souls whose sanctity is so heroic as to qualify them for canonization; it is the heritage of every soul in a state of grace.

When I step outside the confessional after due repentance and the absolution of the priest, I am in a state of grace. At once, then, this blessed union takes effect. Within me is the Holy Spirit, dwelling there— sent, given. As the object of knowledge, He can be experienced by me in a personal and familiar way. I can know Him even as I am known.[19] As the object of love, He becomes my friend, stooping to my level, lifting me to His. At once, then, although still in a merely rudimentary way, the glories of my ultimate reward can dawn upon me. Even upon earth, I have already crossed the threshold of Heaven.

In order for me to enjoy that ultimate vision of God, two things will be necessary for me. First, I shall need to be strengthened so as to survive the splendor and joy of it. No man can see God and live, for, like St. Paul on the road to Damascus, the splendor of the vision would wholly obscure the sight.[20] Just as a tremendous

[19] Cf. 1 Cor. 13:12.
[20] Acts 9:3, 8.

noise will strain the hearing of the ear, or an overbright light will dazzle the eyes to blindness, or an overwhelming joy will break the heart with happiness, so would the vision of God strike with annihilation the poor, weak soul. Hence the light of glory, as it is called by the theologians, has to be brought into use. By this is meant that strengthening of the human faculties which enables them without harm to confront the truth, goodness, power, and beauty of God.

Secondly, this vision implies an immediate contact with God. It is no question simply of faith or hope, but of sight and possession, so that there should be no more veils, no more reproductions or reflections of God, but God Himself.

Those two things sum up what we mean by the Beatific Vision. Now, then, if there is a similarity of kind between that union in Heaven and the union that can be reflected on earth, then grace in this life must play the part of the light of glory in the next, and I must be able, in consequence, to enter into personal relations and immediate contact with God.

Such, then, is the likeness between the indwelling of the Spirit on earth and the Beatific Vision. Wherein comes the difference? The difference, one may say, is largely a difference of consciousness. Here on earth I have so much to distract me that I cannot possibly devote myself in the same way as I shall be able to do then. There are things here that have got to be done, and there is the body itself, which can only stand a certain amount of concentration and intensity. If strained too much, it just breaks down and fails. All this complicates and hampers me.

But in Heaven I shall take on something (of course, a great deal intensified) of the consciousness and alertness of youth. A child can thoroughly enjoy himself, for he has got the happy faculty of forgetting the rest of life, all his troubles, anxieties, and fears. Heaven, then, means the lopping off of all those menaces, and the consequent full appreciation of God in knowledge and love. Hence I must not be disturbed if, here on earth, all these wonderful things which I learn about concerning the indwelling of the Holy Spirit do not seem to take place. It is very unfortunate that I do not appreciate them, but it is something at least to know that they are there. It is a nuisance that I do not see Him, but it is something at least to be certain He is within me.

8

Father, Son, and Holy
Spirit all dwell within us

So far it has been taken for granted that this indwelling is proper to the Holy Spirit, but it must now be added that indeed it is really an indwelling of the Blessed Trinity. It is true that very seldom does Scripture speak of the three Persons as dwelling in the soul, still less of their being given or sent. But every reason for which we attribute this to the Holy Spirit would hold equally well of the other two Persons. By grace we are made partakers of God's divine nature; He comes to us as the object of our knowledge and our love. Why should we suppose that this divine presence applies directly only to the Spirit of God? The only reason, of course, is the impressive wording of the New Testament.

But even here there are equally strong indications that more than the Holy Spirit is implied: "If any man will love me, he will keep my word, and my Father will love him, and we will come to him, and will make our abode with him. . . . But the Paraclete, the Holy Spirit, whom the Father will send in my name: He will teach you all things and bring all things to your mind, whatsoever I shall have said to you."[21] Here, then, it is clearly stated that after our Lord has died, His teaching will be upheld by the Spirit, but that this indwelling will include also the abiding presence of Father and Son.

Why, then, is it repeated so often that the Holy Spirit is to be sent into our hearts, to be given to us, to dwell in our midst? It is for the same reason precisely that we allocate or attribute certain definite acts to the Blessed Persons of the Trinity so as the more easily to discern and appreciate the distinction between Them. In the Creed itself we attribute creation to God the Father Almighty, although we know that Son and Spirit also, with the Father, called the world out of nothingness. Eternity is often, too, looked upon as peculiarly of the Father, although naturally it is common to the Trinity. Note how frequently in the liturgical prayers of the Church comes the expression, "O eternal Father." So

[21]John 14:23, 26.

again, to the Son we attribute wisdom and beauty, turning in our imagination to Him as the Word of God, the figure of His substance, the brightness of His glory. And to the Holy Spirit we more often attribute God's love and God's joy.

All these attributions are attempts to make that high mystery and the three Persons of It alive and distinctive to the human spirit. It is not indeed wholly fancy, but it is the ever active reason endeavoring, for its own better understanding of sacred truths, to give some hint, or find some loophole, whence it shall not be overwhelmed with the greatness of its faith.

Consequently, it must be noted that this indwelling of the Spirit of God is not so absolutely and distinctly proper to God the Holy Spirit, as the Incarnation is proper to God the Son. There the Son, and He alone, became man. It was His personality alone to which was joined, in a substantial union, human nature. But in this present case there is no such unique connection between the soul and the Spirit of God, but it is rather the Ever Blessed Trinity itself that enters into occupation and dwells in the heart.

Of course, that makes the wonder not less, but greater. To think that within the borders of my being is conducted the whole life of the Ever Blessed Three-in-One; that the Father is forever knowing Himself in the Son, and that Father and Son are forever loving themselves in the Spirit; to think that within me are the power and eternity of the Father, whereby creation was called into being, and by whose fiat the visible world will one day break up and fall to pieces; that the wisdom and beauty of the Son, which catch the soul of man as in the meshes of a net, and drove generations of men to a wandering pilgrimage—at the peril of life—to rescue an empty tomb in the wild fury of a crusade; to think that the love of the Holy Spirit, which completes the life of God, and was typified in the tongues of fire and the rush of a great wind at Pentecost;[22] that the power and eternity of the Father, the wisdom and beauty of the Son, and the love and joy of the Spirit are for all time in my heart. Oh, what reverence for my human home of God, reverence alike for soul and body!

[22]Acts 2:1-4.

9

The indwelling of the Holy Spirit fills us with graces

It is very clear that so tremendous a presence as this indwelling implies must have tremendous results. If, as I believe, Father and Son and Spirit are always within me by grace, the effect upon my soul should be considerable. To begin with, the very nearness to God which this indwelling secures must make a great difference to my outlook on life. To have within me the Ever Blessed Trinity is more than an honor; it is a responsibility; it is more than responsibility, for it is the greatest grace of all. To my faith, it makes the whole difference in my attitude to the Mother of God that within her womb for those silent months lay the Incarnate Wisdom. If to touch pitch is to ensure defilement,[23]

[23]Ecclus. 13:1.

to be so close to God is to catch the infection of His divinity.

Or, again, I may have envied, times beyond number, the wonderful grace whereby, upon the breast of his Master, St. John, the beloved disciple, could lovingly lay his head, the joy of so close and so familiar an intimacy with the most beautiful of the sons of men; or I may have pictured the charming scene when He took the dear children of His country on His knees and spoke to them and fondled them so that in His eyes, they could see reflected their own countenances. How life ever after must have been transfigured for them by the memory of that glorious time! Great graces indeed for them all. But what if all life long, by grace, I, too, can be sure of a union even more splendid, an intimacy more lasting, a friendship surpassing the limits of faith and hope?

By grace, then, I receive this indwelling of the Spirit of God, and thereby come into a new and wonderful union with the Ever Blessed Trinity. Now, such a union must have its purpose. Our Lord told us that He was going to send to our hearts the Holy Spirit, an embassy from Heaven to earth conducted by a divine ambassador. The news of the Incarnation and the offer of the motherhood of God were made by means of an angel.[24] But here, in my case, to no created official is this wonderful thing confided, only to God Himself.

That just shows me the importance of the undertaking. In the political world the interests that depend on a diplomatic mission may be easily guessed to be very great when the personnel of the staff is found to contain the highest personages in the country. What deep and abiding interests must then be in question when to my soul comes God the Holy Spirit, sent as the messenger of the Three!

I must consequently expect that the results of this indwelling are judged by God to be considerable, and that it is of great importance to me that, one by one, I should discover them. The Incarnation brought its train of attendant effects which I have to study: the redemption, the sacraments, the sanctifying of all immaterial creation by its union through man with the divinity. This indwelling also must therefore have its effects, the knowledge of which must necessarily make a difference to me in life.

By Baptism comes the beginning of this great grace. As a child, with my senses hardly at all awake to external

[24]Cf. Luke 1:26-35.

He Dwells in Your Soul

life, I had God in my midst. Do I wonder now at the charm of early innocence, when a soul sits silently holding God as its center? It is not that there are dim memories of a pre-existence before birth, but there are always haunting dreams of a true friendship on earth. Baptism, then, begins that early work. At the moment of conversion, when suddenly I was drawn into a tender realization of God's demands and my own heart's hunger, the indwelling of the Spirit became more consciously operative with its flood of light and love.

Since then the sacraments have poured out on me fuller measures of God's grace, and that divine presence therefore should assume larger proportions in my life. I am now the dwelling place of God. When, then, my heart is young, eager, and enthusiastic, let me make Him welcome; and not wait until the only habitation I can offer is in ruins, leaking through an ill-patched roof. A dwelling-place for God! How reverently, then, shall I trust and treasure my body and soul, for they must be as fit as I can make them for the great guest. By reason we learn of Him, by faith we know Him, but by indwelling we taste the sweetness of His presence.

God's loving action within us

10

God's forgiveness restores
our friendship with Him

To understand this first and great effect of grace, I must
know what sin is; and to grasp sin in its fullness, I must
comprehend God. To see the heinousness of what is
done against Him, I must first realize what He is Himself. I have to go through all my ideas of God, my ideas
of His majesty, His power, His tenderness, His justice,
and His mercy. I have got to realize all that He has
done for man before I can take in the meaning of man's
actions against God.

I have to be conscious of the Incarnation; the story
of that perfect life; the privations of it; the culminating
horror of the Passion and death, then of the Resurrec-
tion; the patient teaching of those forty days when He
spoke of the kingdom of God, which He was setting up
on earth; and the Ascension, which did not mean an

end, but only the beginning of His work for men on earth. At once there opened the wonderful stream of graces which flow through the sacraments, and which therefore make His abiding presence continuous upon the world, until its consummation, for the Blessed Sacrament only adds to the wonders of the tenderness and mercy of God. In Heaven, by ever trying to make intercession for us, on earth, by holding out through the sacraments countless ways of grace, this tenderness and mercy shows us something at least of the perfect character of God. Now, it is against one so perfect, so tender, so divine, that sin is committed—a wanton, brutal outrage against an almost overfond love; ingratitude, treachery, and disloyalty united in the basest form.

God is just, as well as merciful, so there has to be an immediate result of sin. Man might see no difference between himself before and after he had sinned; but for all that, a great difference is set up. His soul had been on terms of friendship with God, for it had turned irresistibly to Him, as a flower growing in a dark place turns irresistibly to where the hardy daylight makes its way into the gloom. When a person sins, that friendship is at once broken, for sin means that the soul has deliberately turned its back upon God and is facing the other way, and thus it has been able, by some fatal power, to prevent God's everlasting love from having any effect upon it. God cannot hate; but we can stop His love from touching us.

At once, then, by grievous sin the soul becomes despoiled of its supernatural goods: sanctifying grace, which is the pledge and expression of God's friendship, naturally is banished; charity, which is nothing else than the love of God; the infused virtues; and the gifts are all taken away. Only faith and hope survive, but emptied of their richness of life. Externally no difference; but internally, friendship with God, the right to the eternal heritage, the merits heretofore stored up—all lost. Even God Himself goes out from the midst of the soul, as the Romans heard the voice crying from the temple just before its destruction: "Let us go hence. Let us go hence."

Grace, then, operates to restore all these lost wonders. Sin itself is forgiven; all the ingratitude and disloyalty are put on one side; not simply in the sense that God forgets them, or chooses not to consider them, but in the sense that they are completely wiped away. It is the parable of the Good Shepherd where the sheep is brought back again into the fold, and mixes freely with the others who have never left the presence of their Master.[25] It is the parable of the prodigal son taken back into his father's embrace.[26]

That is what the forgiveness of sin implies. God is once more back again in the soul. He had always been there as the Creator without whose supporting hand the soul would be back in its nothingness; but He is now there again as Father and Master and Friend. Not only the saints who have been endowed with a genius for divine things, but every simple soul that has had its sins forgiven comes at once into that embrace. We are far too apt to look upon forgiveness as a merely negative thing, a removal, a cleansing, and not enough as a return to something great and good and beautiful, the triumphant entrance into our souls of the Father, the Son, and the Spirit.

[25]Cf. Luke 15:4-5; John 10:16.
[26]Luke 15:11-32.

God's forgiveness
completely removes sin

There is something in the forgiveness of sin which implies an element of positive good, and this is called justification. It means that the attitude of God toward forgiven sin is believed by the Catholic Church to be no mere neglect or forgetfulness of its evil, but an actual and complete forgiveness. At the time of the Protestant Reformation a long controversy was waged over this very point, in which the Reformers took up the curious position that forgiveness implied nothing more than that God did not impute sin. He covered up the iniquities of the soul with the blood of His Son, and no longer peered beneath the depths of that sacred and saving sign.

The problem has probably hardly any meaning now, since the original doctrinal principles of Protestantism, the ostensible reasons for the sixteenth-century revolt, have been abandoned long since as hopeless of defense. In fact, all that was really positive in Protestantism has been ruined by its basic negative principle of private judgment. Against such a battering ram Christianity itself is powerless. But that long-forgotten discussion had this much value: it brought out in clear perspective the fullness of the Catholic teaching on the central doctrine of justification and showed its depth and meaning.

Briefly, then, it may be stated that it is not simply that God does not impute evil, but He forgives it. It is as though a rebellion had taken place and its leader had been captured and brought before his offended sovereign. Now, the king might do either of two things if he wished not to punish the culprit. He might simply bid him go off and never appear again, or he might go even further by actually forgiving the rebellion and receiving the rebel back into favor. It is one thing to say that no punishment will be awarded; it is another to say that the crime is forgiven, and that everything is to go on as though nothing had happened. In the first case, we might say that the king chose not to impute the sin; in the other, that he forgave and justified the sinner.

It is just this, then, that the Catholic Church means when She teaches justification as implied in the idea of forgiveness.

It is just this, too, that our Lord meant when He detailed His beautiful parable about the prodigal son. The boy's return home does not mean merely that the father refrains from punishment, but rather that there is a welcome so hearty and so complete that the serious-minded elder brother, coming in from his long labor in the fields, is rather scandalized by its suddenness, and its intensity. Such is indeed God's treatment of the soul. He is so generous, so determined not to be outdone by any sorrow on the part of the sinner, that He overwhelms with the most splendid favors the recently converted soul.

But in this connection we must see in justification a process by which the presence of God is again achieved by man. By sin grace was lost, and with grace went out the Divine Three-in-One; the temple was desecrated, and the veil of the Holy of Holies was utterly rent.[27] Then sin is forgiven, and once more, the sacred home is occupied by God.

[27] Heb. 9:3; Matt. 27:51.

He Dwells in Your Soul

Moreover, when God comes to the soul, He comes with His full strength of love, and thereby gives a new energy and life to man. We love because of some beauty, goodness, or excellence that we see in others. We love, then, because of what is in them. It is their gifts that cause or ignite our love.

But God, who is the only cause, Himself creates excellences by love. We are not loved because we are good; we are good because we are loved, so that this indwelling itself fashions us after God's own heart. "It is the love of God," says St. Thomas, "that produces and creates goodness in things."[28] The divine presence of God in the soul, then, effected by sanctifying grace, makes the soul more worthy a temple, more fit a home. God does not come to us because we are fit, but we are fit because God comes to us.

[28]*Summa Theologica*, I, Q. 20, art. 2.

Our presence with God

12

We can participate in
God's divine nature

The very strong expression *deification* is used by St. Augustine[29] and many of the Fathers to describe one of the effects of grace. By grace we are deified, that is, made into gods. Right at the beginning of all the woes of humanity, when, in the Garden of Eden, Adam and Eve first were tempted, the lying spirit promised that the reward of disobedience would be that they should become "as gods."[30] The result of sin could hardly be that, so man, made only a little lower than the angels,[31] can at times find himself rebuked by the very beasts. Yet the promise became in the end fulfilled, since the

[29]Bishop of Hippo and Doctor of the Church (354-430).
[30]Gen. 3:5.
[31]Cf. Ps. 8:6 (RSV = Ps. 8:5).

Incarnation really effected that transformation, and God, by becoming human, made man himself divine.

St. Peter, in his second letter, insinuates the same truth when he describes the great promises of Christ making us "partakers of the divine nature."[32] The work, then, of grace is something superhuman and divine. Creation pours into us the divine gift of existence and therefore makes us partakers in the divine being, for existence implies a participation in the being of God. The indwelling of the Blessed Trinity, then, does even more, for by it we participate not only in the divine being, but in the divine nature, and we fulfill the prophecy of our Lord: "You are gods."[33] Justification, therefore, is a higher gift than creation, since it does more for us.

This divine participation is what is implied in many texts which allude to the sacrament of Baptism, for the purpose of Baptism is just that: to make us children of God. The phrases concerning "new birth" and "being born again"[34] all are intended to convey the same idea; that the soul, by means of this sacrament, is lifted above

[32] 2 Peter 1:4.
[33] Ps. 81:6 (RSV = Ps. 82:6); John 10:34.
[34] Cf. John 3:3-5.

its normal existence and lives a new life. This life is lived "with Christ in God,"[35] that is, it is a sort of entrance within the charmed circle of the Trinity; or, more accurately, it is that the Blessed Trinity inhabits our soul and enters into our own small life, which at once therefore takes on a new and higher importance. In it henceforth there can be nothing small or mean. For the same reason, our Lord speaks of it to the Samaritan woman as "the gift of God," beside which all His other benefactions fade into nothingness. Again, it is a "fountain of living water," it is a "refreshment," it is "life"[36] itself—not the stagnant water that remains in a pool in some dark wood, but a stream gushing out from its source, fertilizing the ground on every side, soaking through to all the thirsting roots about it, giving freshness and vitality to the whole district through which it wanders. Life, indeed, it bears as its great gift; and so does sanctifying grace carry within it the fertilizing power needed by the soul.

The participation in the divine nature is therefore no mere metaphor, but is a real fact. The indwelling of

[35]Col. 3:3.
[36]Cf. John 4:10-14.

He Dwells in Your Soul

God makes the soul like to God. I find myself influenced by the people with whom I live, picking up their expressions, copying their tricks and habits, following out their thoughts, absorbing their principles, growing daily like them. With God at the center of my life, the same effect is produced, and slowly, patiently, almost unconsciously, I find myself infected by His Spirit. What He loves becomes my ideal; what He hates, my detestation.

But it is even closer than this—no mere concord of wills or harmony of ideas, but a real and true elevation to the life of God. Grace is formally in God, at the back, so to say, of His divine nature, the inner essence of Himself. By receiving it, therefore, I receive something of God and begin to be able to perform divine actions. I can begin to know God even as I am known, to taste His sweetness, and, by His favor, to have personal, experiential knowledge of Him. To act divinely is only possible to those who are made divine. This, then, becomes the formal union with God, its term, its end, its purpose. Therefore, we become deified in our essence by grace, in our intelligence by its light, and in our will by charity.

13

By adoption we are
truly God's children

Here again we have to realize that the sonship of God is
no mere metaphor, no mere name, but a deep and true
fact of huge significance: "Behold what manner of charity the Father hath bestowed upon us, that we should
be called and should be the sons of God!"[37] We become
the sons of God.

St. Paul very gladly quotes the saying of a Greek poet
that men are the offspring of God, making use of a particular word which necessarily implies that both the
begetter and the begotten are of the same nature.[38] A
sonship indeed is what our Lord is Himself incessantly
teaching the Apostles to regard as their high privilege,

[37]1 John 3:1.
[38]Acts 17:28.

for God is not only His Father, but theirs: "Thus shalt thou pray: 'Our Father . . .'"[39] With the Gospels it is in constant use as the view of God that Christianity came especially to teach.

The letters of the New Testament are equally insistent on the same view, for St. Paul is perpetually calling to mind the wonderful prerogatives whereby we cry, "Abba; Father."[40] We are spoken of as co-heirs of Christ, as children of God.[41] St. John, St. Peter, and St. James repeat the same message[42] as the evident result of the Incarnation, for by it we learn that God became the Son of Man, and man the son of God.

Yet it must also be admitted that this sonship of God—which is the common property of all just souls, and is the result of the indwelling of God in the soul— does not mean that we are so by nature, but only by adoption. Now, adoption, as it is practiced by law, implies that the child to be adopted is not already the son, that the new relationship is entered upon entirely at the free choice of the person adopting, and that the

[39]Matt. 6:9.
[40]Gal. 4:6.
[41]Rom. 8:16-17.
[42]John 1:12; 1 Peter 3:22; James 2:5.

child becomes the legal heir to the inheritance of the adopting father.

It is perfectly evident that all these conditions are fulfilled in the case of God's adoption, for we were certainly no children of His before His adoption of us as sons; strangers we were, estranged indeed by the absence of grace and the high gifts of God. Naturally we were made by Him, but had put ourselves far from Him: "You were as sheep going astray."[43] Then this adoption of us by God was indeed and could only have been at His free choice, through no merits of ours, but solely according to the deliberate action of His own will, for "You have not chosen me, but I have chosen you."[44] "So that it is not of him that willeth, nor of him that runneth, but of God that showeth mercy."[45]

Finally, the inheritance is indeed ours by right and title of legal inheritance. We are co-heirs with Christ, and our human nature is lifted up to the level of God—not, of course, that we supplant Him who is by nature the true Son of God, but that we are taken into

[43]1 Peter 2:25.
[44]John 15:16.
[45]Rom. 9:16.

partnership with Him, and share in Him the wonderful riches of God.

Here, then, I may learn the worth and dignity of the Christian name. I am a true son of God, and what else matters upon earth? I have indeed to go about my life with its vocation and all that is entailed in it. I have to work for my living, it may be, or take my place in the family, or lead my own solitary existence. I have to strive to be efficient and effective in the material things of life that fall to my share to be done. But it is this sonship of God that alone makes any matter in the world.

In our own time we have heard a very great deal about culture and the ultimate value of the world, but we have seen also to what evil end so fine a truth may lead men. True culture is not a question of scientific attainments, or mechanical progress, or the discovery of new inventions of destruction, or even of medical and useful sciences, but true culture is the perfect and complete development of the latent powers of the soul. True culture may indeed make use of sciences and art; perhaps in its most complete sense science and art are needed for the most finished culture of which man is capable; but it is in its very essence the deepening of man's truest desire, the full stretch of his widest flights of fancy, the achievement of his noblest ideals. What nobler ideal, or fancy, or desire, can a man have than to be called and to be the son of God; to know that he has been drawn into the close union of God; to feel within his very essence the presence of God; to have personal experience as the objects of his knowledge and love of the Father, Son, and Spirit?

14

We are heirs to a divine kingdom

One of the conditions of adoption is that the newly chosen son should become the legal heir of the new father. Without this legal result or consequence, adoption has no meaning. Merely to get a boy to enter a family circle does not imply adoption, for this last has a distinct meaning with a distinct purpose. If, then, we are the heirs of God, we are really possessed of a right to His divine inheritance. Heaven has been made indeed our home. We speak of it in our hymns as *patria*, which we can translate as the "land of our fathers." We claim it thereby in virtue of our parentage, and our parentage is of God.

If, then, He is our Father, not by nature, but by adoption—that is, by grace—we are nonetheless His heirs and have some sort of right over His possessions and riches. A father cannot, without leave of his adopted son, alienate any of the family heirlooms; the adopted son now, by the father's own free act, acquires, not indeed dominion over the riches of the home, but, at any rate, an embargo on the father's free exercise of those riches. He could even demand, against his father, a legal investigation into the due use and investment of them. His signature is required for every document that relates to them. He has become almost a part-owner of his father's possessions, since he is their legal heir.

All this is implied by adoption in its true sense, and therefore it must be intended to apply to us when we are spoken of as God's adopted sons.

I can, therefore, truthfully speak of myself as an heir of God. Of course, I cannot mean that there is any possible question of "the death of the testator," that is, of God. That is quite clearly of no significance here. But adoption does give me some sort of claim to the heritage of God. Now, the law defines a heritage as that by which a man is made rich. It includes not the riches only, but also the source of the riches, so that if I have a claim to God's riches, I have a claim also upon the source of those riches. For the heir is entitled not merely to a legacy, but to the whole of the fortune. I have a right to the whole fortune of God, to the whole universe. At once, as soon as I realize it, the whole of the world is mine. This is the doctrine of the mystics that, misunderstood, led astray the communists of the Middle Ages. These claimed a common ownership of the wealth of all the world, whereas what was intended was that we should look upon the whole world as ours.

To me, then, in life, nothing can be strange or distant or apart. No places can there be where my mind cannot enter and roam at will and feel at home; no things can be profane, no people who are not tabernacles of God, no part of life that is not steeped in that living presence. The only possible boundary is the love and the grace of God. There will indeed come evil frontiers beyond which my soul could never dwell. But all else is of God and is therefore my right. All creation is mine; the wonder and beauty of it, life and death, pleasure and pain alike yield up to me their secrets and disclose the hidden name of God.

Here, then, I can find that divine wealth that God, by His adoption of us, intends us to inherit. Wherever I turn, I shall find Him. Whether life has smooth ways or rough, whether it hangs my path with lights or hides me in gloom, I am the heir to all that earth or sea or sky can boast of as their possession. Indeed, these are only the rich things of God, whereas I have a claim upon even more. I have a claim upon the very source of this wealth, that is, upon God Himself, for He is the sole source of all His greatness. I have a right to God Himself. He is mine. He who holds in the hollow of His hands the fabric of the world, who with His divine power supports, and with His Providence directs, the intricate pattern of the world, has Himself by creation entered deeply into the world; at the heart of everything He lies hidden. But even more by grace, He comes in a fuller, richer way into the depths of the soul. Here in me are Father, and Son, and Spirit.

Dear God, teach me to understand the wonder of this indwelling, to appreciate its worth, to be thankful for its condescension, to reverence its place of choice, to be conscious of its perpetual upholdings.

By this indwelling, I am an heir to the fullness of the Divine riches. By it I, a creature, possess in His fullness my Creator, Redeemer, and Lord.

We must yield
completely to God

I have God the Holy Spirit with me. He comes to me in order that I may surrender myself to Him. Of course I cannot merge my personality in His to the extent of having no power of my own, but God has such infinite dominion over the heart of man that He is able to move the will, without in any sense whatever violating its freedom.

In the Liturgy of the Church, there are two or three prayers which speak about God "compelling our rebellious wills." Now for anyone else to "compel my will" would be to destroy it as a will, since, as even Cromwell[46] freely confessed, "The will suffereth no compulsion." I

[46]Oliver Cromwell (1599-1658), English revolutionary leader and Lord Protector of England.

cannot be made to will against my will. That would be a contradiction, although I can be made to *act* against my will, for my actions do not necessarily imply that my will is in them. But even though no one else can move my will without utterly destroying my moral freedom, God can, for He is intimate to the will and moves it, not really as an external, but as an internal, power. St. Thomas Aquinas repeatedly refers to this and says over and over again the same thing—namely, that God is so intimately united to man, and so powerful, that can He not only move man to will, but also move him to will freely by affecting, not only the action of man, but also the very mode of the action.[47]

Such is man, whether in a state of grace or not, that his will is in the hands of God, to be moved by man freely, but not so as to exclude God's movement.

Naturally enough it is far easier to say this than to explain it. Indeed the mere statement is all that is actually binding upon faith, and the particular explanation favored by St. Thomas, in his general acceptance of St. Augustine's teaching, assumes for us deep and abiding importance on account of the very clear reasons given

[47]*Summa Theologica*, I, Q. 105, art. 4; I-II; Q. 9, art. 6.

and the great authority of his name; but in any case, there is something far more special in the guidance of the Holy Spirit sought for by the soul in its endeavor to "live godly in Christ Jesus."[48] It has to yield itself to the promptings of God, be eager to catch His every whisper and quick in its obedience to His every call.

For this to be achieved, the first work is an emptying of the soul. Every obstacle has to be gotten rid of; any attachment to creatures that obscures God's light has to be broken through (although not every attachment to creatures, since, unless I love man, whom I see, I cannot possibly know what love means when applied to God, nor can I suppose myself to be able to understand or love God, whom I do not see[49]). First, then, I must cleanse my soul by leveling and smoothing and clearing its surface and depths.

Then I must yield myself into His arms. I shall not know very often the way He wishes me to go. It may be only one step at a time, and then darkness again; or I may be taken swiftly and surely and openly along a clear road. That is His business, not mine, but I must

[48]2 Tim. 3:12.
[49]Cf. 1 John 4:20.

be prepared to be not always able to follow the meaning of what He wants of me. It is not necessary at all that I should know. If I am faithful and loyal and full of trust, things will gradually settle themselves, and I shall at least be able to look back and understand the significance and purpose of many things that at first appeared accidental, and even in opposition to the end I considered God had in view for me.

Thus by looking back I can sometimes get a shrewd idea of what is to follow; but often it is only a guess, nothing more than that. Still, generally, it would seem that people who surrender themselves to God do get a sense or a feeling which leads them right and makes them sure. It is the divine tenderness stooping to poor, muddled humanity and making it transfigured with God's own glory. The advance, then, whether consciously grasped or not, is in due proportion to the purity and fidelity of the soul—purity in its act of cleansing, fidelity in its subjection to the promptings of the Holy Spirit.

God's gifts within us

16

God's gifts make us
aware of His guidance

To live the spiritual life to its fullness we need the instinctive governance of the Holy Spirit. All day long, and even all through the hours when consciousness is asleep, the Holy Spirit is speaking to us in many ways. He is offering us His heavenly counsel, enlightening our minds to an ever more complete understanding of the deep truths of faith, and generally imparting to us that deep knowledge without which we cannot advance.

Reason and common sense have their own contribution to make in opening our minds and hearts to a proper interpretation of all that is about us and within us; but reason and common sense have to be supernaturalized themselves, to be illumined by the light of a far higher plane of truth. Hence the need of this divine instinct is patent to anyone who considers the purpose and destiny of the soul. But it is difficult at times to understand and to grasp surely the words of divine wisdom, since, by sin's coarseness, the refinement of the soul is dulled and rendered but little responsive; or, rather, it is not so much a matter of being responsive to a message as primarily of hearing and understanding it. It seems to be very obvious that God must be speaking to me almost without ceasing; it is equally obvious that very little of this is noticed.

Here, then, I am in the world and needing the governance of God's instinct. Here, too, is this whispered counsel and enlightenment of God, perpetually being made to me. Yet, although made by God, and needed by me, this counsel and enlightenment, I can be certain, must frequently be entirely lost to me. It is as though I lived in a perfectly beautiful country, with stretching landscape about, and beautiful glimpses of hills and woodland, and yet never saw or appreciated the view; as though heavenly music were about me, to which I never paid the slightest attention; as though my best-loved friend stood by me and I never lifted my eyes, and so did not know of his presence. Of course, it is really a great deal worse than that, for I do not need with an absolute necessity the view or the music, or the friend, whereas I do most certainly need this divinely offered help, guidance, and enlightenment.

Hence it is clear that neither my need nor God's instinct suffices. Something else is required by means of which I am able to make use of that instinct, to hear its message, to discover its meaning, to apply its advice to myself, otherwise am I no better than a general who possesses the full plan of his allies, in all its details, but written in a cipher that he cannot read.

To produce this reaction or perception is the work of the sevenfold gifts. They are habits infused into the soul, which strengthen its natural powers, and make them responsive to every breath of God and capable of heroic acts of virtue. By the gifts, my eyes are made able to see what had been hidden; my ears quick to catch what had not been heard. The gifts do not, so to say, supply eye or ear, but make more delicate, refined, and sensitive the eye and ear already there. Their business is to intensify rather than to create powers established in me by grace. Less excellent necessarily than the theological virtues which unite me to God, they are yet more excellent than the other virtues, although, being rooted in charity and thereby linked up among themselves, they are also part of the dowry that charity brings in her train.

He Dwells in Your Soul

On this account it is clear that, from the moment of Baptism, the sevenfold gifts are the possession of the soul, and whosoever holds one, holds all. Yet by the sacrament of Confirmation, it would appear certain that something further is added, some more delicate perception, some livelier sensitiveness; or it may be, as other theologians point out, that by Confirmation these gifts are more steadily fixed in the soul, more fully established, more firmly held. But in any case, it is clear what they are to me: habits whereby I am perfected to obey the Holy Spirit of God.

17

Being attuned to God leads to acts of virtue

The possession of the sevenfold gifts results in the performance of certain virtuous acts, for it is perfectly obvious that if I am so blessed by the gifts, that I find my reason, will, and emotions made increasedly perceptive of divine currents previously lost to me, I can hardly help acting in a new way. I now discover the view about me, and the music, and, consequently, my manner of life must in some ways be different from before. The vision has come; it cannot simply open my eyes to new things in life without thereby altering that very life itself. Not only shall I find that what seemed to me before to be evil now appears to me to be a blessing; but on that very account, what before I tried to avoid, or, having got, tried to be rid of, I shall now accept, perhaps even seek. Similarly, whereas then I was weak, now I am strong; and increase of strength means new activities, new energy put into the old work and finding its way into works altogether new. My emotions, finally, which imperiled and dominated my life, slip now into a subordinate position and, while thereby as actively employed as before, are held under discipline. It is clear, therefore, that the gifts will not leave me where I was before, but will influence my actions as well as alter my vision.

I find, then, that these new habits will develop into new activities. But this means also that I have a new idea as to the means of achieving the full happiness of life. Once upon a time I thought happiness meant comfort; now I see that it means something quite different. My view of happiness has changed. I am therefore obliged to change also my idea as to the means and conditions whereby, and in which, happiness can be found. I had attempted to climb out of my valley over the hills in the west; I now attempt to climb over the hills to the east. The steps by which once I clambered are useless to me. I must try new ones in the opposite hills.

Just that is what our Lord meant by promulgating His Beatitudes.[50] These are just the new blessedness, so

[50]Matt. 5:3-12.

to say, which results from realizing that happiness now means the knowledge and love of God. Things that previously I fled from, I now seek; things once my bugbear, are now the objects of my delight. Poverty, meekness, mourning, the hunger and thirst for justice, cleanness of heart, the making of peace, mercy, and the suffering of persecution for justice's sake are now found to be the steps to be passed over, the conditions to be secured before happiness can be finally secured.

These things, then, are beatitudes to me. They are acts which I finally achieve by means of the new enlightenment gained through the gifts of God. Actively I am merciful and meek and clean of heart. I perform these actions, and they are the result of visions seen, and counsels heard, through the new sensitiveness to the divine instinctive guidance that of old passed me by without finding in my heart any response. To be forever pursuing peace and sorrow and, at whatever cost, justice, is now an energizing state of life which is due entirely to the new perception of the value of these things, so that we are right in asserting that the Beatitudes are nothing else than certain actions, praised by our Lord and practiced by us as a result of the establishment in our souls of seven definite habits. But not only

He Dwells in Your Soul

are they actions; they produce as an effect joy in the heart, for which reason we call them "beatitudes." They show me what is truly blessed and thereby give me, even here on earth, a foretaste of the bliss of final happiness.

18

God's gifts refresh and
strengthen our souls

Besides the Beatitudes there are other acts that follow from the gifts when properly used by the soul. The Beatitudes are means which, under the light infused by God, are valued at their true worth as leading finally to happiness in its more complete sense. But when these are thus put into practice—for the soul understands the new meaning life gathers—they do not end the wonders of the action of grace.

As a boy I met life and found it full of interest and dawning with the glories of success. The world in its aspect of nature had such manifest beauties that these quickly entranced and thrilled the soul. The sun and grass and flowers and woods and waters make no secret of their kinship with their creator; the English poet Francis Thompson found them "garrulous of God," so garrulous in our youth that we see that life is full of very good things.

Then comes the reaction (to many before full manhood), when life is found to be full of illusion. Life is now judged a melancholy business, apt to fail you just when the need of it is most discovered, and hard to be certain of. It is the age of romantic melancholy, when most people put into verse their sorrow at the disappointment to be found in all things of beauty. Every tree and flower and "dear gazelle" is no sooner loved than it is lost through death or misunderstanding.

Then, finally, the balance is set right. The two phases pass. They are both true only as half-truths. There is no denying that life is good and beautiful and thrilling. The boy's vision is correct. Yet it is equally true to say that there is sorrow and suffering and death and disappointment in all human things. But a new phase, blessedly a last phase, dawns upon the soul. Sorrow and pain are real, but the old happiness of boyhood is made to fit in and triumph over them by the sudden realization that strength is the lesson to be learned. Sorrow comes so that discipline may be born in the soul, and self-restraint and humility. Life is hard, but its very hardness is no evil, but our means of achieving good.

That is the very atmosphere of the Beatitudes, the message they bring, the teaching they imparted from the Sermon on the Mount. Poverty, cleanness of heart, mercy, and meekness are all things difficult to acquire, but they give a real, true blessedness to the soul that will see their value. Life is no longer a disappointment, but the training ground of all good.

Finally, there follow other acts, too many to number, although there are twelve usually given, which result from gifts and beatitudes. They are: charity, joy, peace, patience, benignity, goodness, longanimity, mildness, faith, modesty, continency, and chastity.[51] These are called the fruits of the Holy Spirit, for they represent in that metaphorical sense the ultimate result of the gifts. They are the last and sweetest consequences of the sevenfold habits infused by the Spirit.

Trees are grown in an orchard for their fruits, and therefore it can be said that the fruit is, from the gardener's point of view, the purpose for which the tree is cultivated (for of the fruitless fig, our Lord asked why it cumbered the ground[52]). Similarly, these fruits of the

[51]Gal. 5:22-23.
[52]Cf. Luke 13:7.

He Dwells in Your Soul

Holy Spirit can be looked upon as the very purpose for which the gifts were given—that I might, by seeing a new blessedness in life's very troubles, begin to find joy and peace and patience and faith, where before I had found only sorrow. Endlessly could the list of these fruits be extended, for St. Paul has chosen only a very few; but these that he names are what a man delights in when he has received the gifts, and has understood and valued the Beatitudes. Sweetness is what they add to virtue—ease, and comfort. I not only hunger and thirst for justice, but enjoy the very pain of the pursuit.

19

We can know God
through His creation

This gift of God illumines and perfects the intelligence. The purpose of the gifts, it has been already explained, is to make the soul more alive to, and more appreciative of, the whispered impetus of God; not to create new faculties, but to increase the power of those already existing. My mind, then, has to be supernaturalized and refined to that pitch of perception which will enable it to grasp and to understand God's message.

Now, the mind itself works upon a great variety of subjects. It has whole worlds to conquer, planes of thought which are very clearly distinguishable. Yet in its every activity, it needs this divine refinement, so that in all, four gifts are allotted to perform this complete enlightenment of the mind: knowledge, understanding, wisdom, and counsel.

He Dwells in Your Soul

Knowledge overcomes ignorance and is concerned with the facts, visible and sense-perceived, in creation; for by the council of the Vatican it is laid down as part of the deposit of faith that human reason can prove the existence of God altogether apart from the supernatural motives which grace supplies.[53] The visible world is held to contain ample proofs which in themselves are adequate logically to convince human understanding of the existence of God. Individual reason may fail to satisfy itself. People may declare truthfully that they are not convinced; the Church insists only that it can be done.

Knowledge, however, in this sense, is a gift of God whereby we discover Him in His own creation and in the works of man. It is here no mere task set to reason for detecting the Creator in His handiwork, but an actual vision by which the soul is supernaturalized and sees Him patently everywhere. The beauteous face of nature is merely seen as a veil, hiding a beauty more sublime. Things of dread as well as things of loveliness come into the scheme, things trivial and things tremendous, things majestic and things homely, all that

[53]Cf. Vatican Council I, can. 2, sect. 1: DS 3026.

We can know God through His creation

God has made. Even the work of man, who is himself only one of the greater masterpieces of the Great Artisan, is affected by this new light with which the world is flooded.

The delicate pieces of machinery constructed by human ingenuity, that grow ever greater in wonder and in power, are themselves still God's work once removed; they are the fruits of a mind that He has constructed, and they do not exhaust the capacity of that mind. They reveal hidden potentialities as well as express actual achievements. Weapons of destruction, with all the horror they rightly inspire, are yet witnesses again to that parent-intelligence whence was begotten man himself. As soon as it is considered, all this, of course, is admitted by every believer in God, but the gift of knowledge makes it realized and seen steadfastly.

Life, then, of itself is full of illusion. That is the cry, desolating and pitiful, which arises from the higher followers of every religious faith. Man is bound to the wheel; his mind is compassed with infirmity; he is born into ignorance. Desire tumultuously hustles all his days. He needs, therefore, some light whereby he may find the true inner meaning of all with which he comes in contact.

He Dwells in Your Soul

Here, then, in the gift of knowledge is such a true vision—understanding, vouchsafed him of the visible things of creation. He will realize as much, perhaps even more than before, the attraction of beauty, only it will be no snare, but a beckoning light. He will find in it illusion, but the perfect image of a greater beauty. The charm of the world about him will become greater; the wonders of nature, the intricate pattern of mechanical appliances, the fury of storms, the tumult of the wind, the terrific force of pestilence, the psychological facts of man's mind, the construction of his frame, the grouping of his social instincts: all now will be alive with God, shot through with the divine splendor, elevated to His order of life, eloquent of His name—because of a deepening knowledge of God achieved through a knowledge of His creatures.

20

Understanding penetrates
the truths of the Faith

There is another gift required to perfect the intelligence when it is engaged upon the principles of truth.
The mind was created by God to exercise itself upon
truth: primarily, the Supreme Truth; secondarily, all
truths which, by their essence, must themselves be ra-
diations from the Supreme Truth. These truths are of
endless variety, both in their relationship to each other
and in the particular line in which they operate.

They are the truths of arts and science, the intricate
yet unchanging laws that govern the growth and development of matter, the complicated processes whereby
organic beings build up their tissues and multiply themselves by means of the cell principle. There are again
the curious laws, as they are called, that affect gravita-
tion, that have to be counted upon in the science of

architecture, and in all the various kindred crafts of man. There are principles, too, that underlie the whole series of the arts, principles of truth and life and beauty. Upon these the mind must feed, and in them all, the mind must be able to trace the character and being of God.

But there are also far higher truths that are taught only by Revelation, safeguarded by authority, and grouped under the title of faith. These truths are higher than the others, since they directly concern a higher being, that is, God. All truths are truths about God, but the truths of faith concern themselves immediately with the being, life, and actions of God. Understanding, therefore, is the gift perfecting the mind for these.

It might seem, perhaps, that the light of faith is itself sufficient, and that no further gift were needed, since it is the very purpose of faith to make us accept this revelation of God, enlightening and strengthening the intelligence until, under the dominion of the will, it says: "I believe." It is true that faith suffices for this, but we require something more than faith, or at least if we do not absolutely require more, we shall progress more rapidly and further when we are not only able to believe but to understand. In every article of faith, there is always something which is mysterious or hidden, some obscurity due not to the entanglement of facts, but to the weakness of the human mind. Of course, this must to some extent always exist, for man can never hope to comprehend God until, by the Beatific Vision, he sees Him face to face; but a good deal of the obscurity can be lifted by the mere operation of the mind under the light of God, not arising purely from study, but from the depth of love enkindled by God. It is a commonplace in the lives of the saints that without instruction they still manage to learn the deep mysteries of God; the same is true of many simple souls whom we meet from time to time in the world. They not only believe, but penetrate the truths of faith.

Here, then, I have ready to hand a most useful gift of God. I desire not only to believe, but to absorb and to penetrate the mysteries of God. I want to taste to the full the meaning of life as a whole, to develop every power that lies in me, to make the truths of revelation blossom out ever more fully, till their hidden and mystical significance becomes gradually more clear. The pages of Holy Scripture are full of instruction, but they will not yield up their secrets save to a soul attuned to God. That can be effected by the gift of understanding.

He Dwells in Your Soul

I shall find by its means that these treasures are inexhaustible, that from mere abstract teaching, the sayings of the Master and His Apostles become full of practical meaning, that all life about me takes on a new and richer significance. History and social life open their doors to whoever has this blessed gift, and it becomes clearly seen that their maker and builder is God. The dullness of souls who will not believe, or only believe and then stop short, becomes painful to note and bothersome to put up with, but this is the price one has to pay for so fine a vision. By this, then, we peer into the depths of faith, and find them gradually and steadily growing more and more clear and penetrable.

21

Wisdom sees as God sees

All writers on the gifts of the Holy Spirit place wisdom as the highest gift of all. It takes this high position partly because its work is done in the intelligence, which is man's highest power, and partly because it is that highest power occupied to its highest capacity.

Like knowledge and understanding, its business is to make us see God everywhere, in the material and spiritual creation of God, in the concrete facts of existence, and in the revealed truths of faith. It produces in a soul a sense of complete certainty and hope.

Hence wisdom is sometimes described as neighbor to hope; indeed, its finest side is often just that determined and resolute conviction with which the soul rises above every possible disaster, and is prepared to brave every contingency in its sureness of God's final power and the efficacy of His will. It comes closer, therefore, to God Himself than to either understanding or knowledge. Understanding and knowledge do, indeed, enable the soul to be continuously conscious of the divine presence—of God immanent as well as transcendent, God in the heart of the world as well as wholly above the world—and they affect this consciousness by enabling the soul to see Him everywhere. They lift the veil. They show His footprints. They trace everywhere the marks of His power, wisdom, and love. But it is noticeable that they lead to God from the world. I see a flower, and by the gift of knowledge I am immediately aware of the author of its loveliness; by understanding I perceive with clearness the wonder of God's working in the world. By knowledge and understanding I lift my eyes from earth to Heaven; by wisdom I look from Heaven to see the earth.

Wisdom, therefore, implies an understanding of the world through God, whereas knowledge and understanding suppose a perception of God through the world. Wisdom takes its stand upon causes, the other two upon effects. Knowledge and understanding work from creatures to Creator; wisdom looks upon all the world through the eyes of God. Consequently the effect of wisdom is that the soul sees life as a whole. Matter and truth are to it no longer separate planes of thought, but one. There is at once no distinction between them in the eyes of God, for both are manifestations of Himself and creatures of His making.

Hence the soul that is endowed with wisdom climbs up to God's own height, and looking down upon the world, sees it "very good,"[54] noticing how part fits in with part, and how truths of faith and truths of science, how sunset and flower and Hell are linked one with another to form the pattern of God's design. Each has its place in the divine economy of God's plan; each is equally of God, equally sharing in His purposes, although some are able to express God better than others. The effect, then, is largely that the whole of life is coordinated, and "equality, fraternity, liberty"[55] becomes the motto, not of a revolution, but of the ordered government of God.

The opposite to this gift is folly, for a man who fails in wisdom loses all true judgment of the values of human life. He is perpetually exchanging the more for the less valuable, bestowing huge gifts in just barter, as

[54]Gen. 1:31.
[55]The motto of the French Revolution.

he imagines, for what is merely showy and trivial. Not by causes, but by effect does he consider life and its activities.

The wise man, then, estimates everything by its highest cause. He compares and discovers, gleans the reason of God's Providence, its purpose, its fitness. First principles are his guide, not the ready and practical proverbs that display the wit and worldly wisdom of the lesser man. Eternity becomes of larger moment than time, since time is merely for eternity. God's law is more convincing than man's, for man's enactments are not laws at all when they come in conflict with divine commands. Faith is so deeply in him that he judges between propositions, and discovers truth against heresy. He has climbed to the heights of God and sees all the world at his feet, and knows it as God knows it, the world and its Lord and the glory of it.

22

Counsel guides our decisions

The fourth gift that perfects the intelligence acts rather as a moderating than as a stimulating influence. The soul is often impetuous in its decisions, moved by human feelings and passions, urged by desire, love, hatred, prejudice. Quickly stirred to action, it dashes into its course without any real attention to, or understanding of, its better wisdom. Frequently in life my lament has to be that I acted on the impulse of the moment.

There is so much that I am sorry for, not merely because now I see what has actually resulted, but because, even then, I had quite sufficient reason to let me be certain what would result. I was blind, not because my eyes could not have seen, but because I gave them no leave to see. I would not carefully gaze at the difficulties, not puzzle out in patience what would most likely be the result. Even my highest powers are often my most perilous guides, since, moved by generosity, I engaged myself to do what I have no right to perform, and find that I have in the end been generous not only with what is my own, but sometimes with what belongs to another, not as though I deliberately gave away what belonged to another, but just because I had no deliberation at all. I need, then, the Holy Spirit of God to endow me with the gift of counsel, which corresponds to prudence.

Now prudence, which counsel helps and protects, is eminently a practical gift of God, not so high as wisdom, not so wonderful in the beauty of its vision as knowledge or understanding, yet for all a most important and homely need. The other intellectual gifts of the Spirit are more abstract. They give us just the whisper of God that enables us to see the large ways of God in the world. They give, in consequence, the great principles that are to govern us in life. Hence their importance is very great. We do so seriously need to know by what principles we are to measure life's activities, on what basis to build up the fabric of our souls, to be sure that God's laws are very clearly and definitely made manifest to us.

But, after all, that is only one-half of the difficulty, for even after I know the principles of action, I have still the trouble—in some ways more full of possibilities of mistake—of applying them to concrete experience. I know that sacrifice is the law of life; I know that meekness over-indulged may be cowardice; I know that I may sin by not having anger: that is all evident, a series of platitudes. But here, and now, have I come to the limit of meekness? Must I manifest my angry protests? Am I obliged to attend to my own needs and renounce the idea of sacrifice? There daily are questions that puzzle, torture, and bruise me with scruples.

Just here, then, I have intense need for this practical gift of God in order with nicety and precision to apply principles to concrete cases; often I am precipitate or perhaps dilatory. I am in a hurry or cannot make up my mind—shall I answer those who attack me, or shall I be silent? Our Lord was silent and made answer by turns. Counsel, then, is my need from God, the instinct whereby a practical judgment is quickly and safely made. All the more have I a tremendous need for this if my life is full of activity, if pressure of work, or social life, or the demands of good and useful projects, or the general tendency of my family surroundings make my day crowded and absorbed, for the very combined and concentrated essence of life will need some exceedingly moderate influence to produce any sense of balance or proportion in my judgment. The people about me I notice to become more and more irritable, mere creatures of impulse. I feel some such malign influence invading the peaceful sanctuary of my soul, disturbing its even outlook on things, driving out my serene calm. I must anchor on to this gift of God, become prudent, detached, filling my mind with the counsel of the Holy Spirit.

23

Fortitude strengthens our will

After the intelligence comes the will, which also, because of the very large part it plays in all human action,
needs to be perfected by a gift of the Spirit. It is necessary to repeat that the Holy Spirit does not, by His
gifts, bestow on the soul new powers and new faculties, but develops, refines, and perfects faculties already
there. It is not the creation of new eyes to see new visions, but the strengthening of the eyes of the soul so as
to see more clearly and with a longer sight.

The will, then, has also to be strengthened, for it is
the will that lies at the very heart of all heroism. Merely
to have a glimpse of greatness is but part of a hero's
need. No doubt it is a larger part, for very many of us
never by instinct at all touch on the borders of greatness; we do not see or understand how in our little lives
we can be great; we have not the imagination lit up by

He Dwells in Your Soul

God, no vision; yet "when the vision fails, the people shall perish."[56] But even when that sudden showing does, by God's mercy, come to us, we still fall far short of it. It is too high, too ideal, too far removed from weak human nature to seem possible to us. That is to say, our will has failed us. We are faced by some huge obstacle, or even by a persistent refusal to budge, on behalf of someone (ourselves or another), to go forward and to do; we struggle, fail, lose heart, surrender, cease our efforts. What do we want? Fortitude, that "persistive constancy" that to Shakespeare[57] was the greatest quality of human wills.

How is this achieved? By appreciating the nearness of God to us. The gifts make us responsive to God with an ease and instantaneousness that operates smoothly and without friction. That is God's doing, not ours. He gives us this wonderful power of being able to register at once every passing inspiration. The gifts that refine the intelligence allow it to perceive sights which before were hidden. The gift that refines the will must do this by some kindred action. Now, for overcoming the

[56]Cf. Prov. 29:18 (King James Version).
[57]William Shakespeare (1564-1616), English playwright.

difficulties that beset the will, strength is needed. Therefore the will must be refined by being made strong.

How can the will be made strong by the Holy Spirit? What exactly happens to its mechanism to secure for it the power of endurance? The easiest way of understanding how this effect is brought about is to suppose that the soul by its refinement, by that delicacy whereby it responds instantly to a divine impression, is quickly aware of God's nearness to it. It perceives how close it is to the Spirit of God, and the sense of this nearness makes it better able to hold on to its duty. In the old style of warfare we often read of wives and mothers coming to the field of battle that their presence might awake their men to the topmost pitch of courage. Even in the modern methods of fighting, the moral effect of the presence of the emperor or king is considered to have an effect upon the troops. Of course, in the case of the Holy Spirit it is more homely since His familiar presence strengthens and inspires by love, trust, and sympathy.

For this reason the name Comforter, in its original sense of strengthening, becoming the fort of the soul, was given to the Holy Spirit; and the result is that the recipient is able to hold on or, in our modern slang, to carry on. By nature so many of us are prone to seek our own comforts at the expense of what we know to be the higher side of us. Human respect makes us again cowardly, or the sheer monotony of perseverance dulls and wearies the soul. We get so depressed with the strain of making efforts that we are very much inclined to let the spiritual side of life go under, or at least be rendered as little heroic as possible, for it is real heroism even just to go on. The silent pressure of temptations, when their passion and fury have died down, is a constant worry, an unconscious weight on the mind like the thought of war that lies heavily at the back of the consciousness of those whose external lives seem empty of war reminders. We want to be courageous and fearless, to undergo. Then we must hold fast to God's nearness to us, and feel the virtue going out from Him to us, although He does but touch the hem of our garments by His indwelling.[58]

[58]Cf. Mark 5:27-30.

24

Piety moves us to love God

Besides our intelligence and will, we have other faculties that go by a diversity of names; sometimes they are called the emotions, sometimes the passions, and sometimes they are alluded to as the sentimental side of our nature. But by whatever name we may happen to call them, it is clear that they represent just those movements of our being which are not really rational in themselves, although they can be controlled by the reason. It is simplest to divide them into two classes and to realize that they lie just on the borderline between spirit and matter, partly of soul, partly of body. These two classes are arranged according as the emotion attracts or repels man. The repelled emotions are fear, anger, hatred, etc.; the attracted are love, desire, joy, etc.

The gift of piety enables even the emotions to be made responsive to God. It is always the notion of some perfect instrument which must be made harmonious that perhaps most clearly shows us the work of the Holy Spirit in the gifts of God—some perfect instrument which needs to be so nicely attuned that its every string shall give out a distinct note, and shall require the least movement from the fingers of God's right hand to make its immediate response. Here, then, we have first to record the fact that the purpose of this gift is to make the emotions of passions so refined, so perfectly strung, that at once the slightest pressure of the divine instinct moves them to turn their love, desire, and joy toward God, finding in Him the satisfaction of their inmost heart.

Piety, in its Latin significance (and here in theology, of course, we get almost all our terms through the Latin tongue), means the filial spirit of reverence toward parents. Virgil gives to the hero of his Roman epic[59] the repeated title of pious, because he wishes always to emphasize Aeneas's devotion to his aged father. Hence it is clear that what is primarily intended here is that we should be quickly conscious of the fatherhood of God. The medieval mystics, especially our English ones like

[59]Virgil (Roman poet; 70-19 B.C.), *The Aeneid*.

Richard Rolle of Hampole,[60] and Mother Julian of Norwich,[61] curiously enough were fond of talking about the motherhood of God in order to bring out the protective and devoted side of God's care for us.

Of course, God surpasses both a mother's and father's love in His ineffable love for us. But then it is just that sweetness of soul in its attitude toward God, that this gift produces in me a readiness to perceive His love in every turn of fortune, and to discover His gracious pity in His treatment of my life. It requires a divine indwelling of the Spirit of God to effect this in my soul, for although I may be, by nature, easily moved to affection, prompt to see and profit by every opening for friendship, yet I must, no less, have a difficulty in turning this into my religious life without God's movement in my soul.

Perhaps the most unmistakable result of this is in the general difference between predominantly Catholic nations and non-Catholic ones in their ideas of religion. Even if one takes a non-Catholic nation at its best and a Catholic nation at its worst, the gulf between them is

[60]English hermit and mystic (c. 1300-1349).
[61]English mystic (c. 1342-1413).

enormous, for at its lowest, the religion of the Catholic nation will be attractive at least with its joy, and the non-Catholic repellent with gloom. There is a certain hardness about all other denominations of Christianity, a certain restrained attitude of awe toward God, which although admirable in itself, is perfectly hateful when it is made the dominant note in religion. Better joyous superstition than gloomy correctness of worship; better—far better—to find happy children who have little respect, and much comradeship toward their parents, than neat and quiet children who are in silent awe of their parents.

It is, then, to develop this side of religion that the gift of piety is given. The result, then, is a sweetness, a gracefulness, a natural lovingness toward God and all holy persons and things, as opposed to a gloomy, respectable, awkward, self-conscious hardness toward our Father in Heaven. Clever, trained people have most to be on their guard, for the intellectual activities of the soul are apt to crowd out the gentler, simpler side of character.

25

Reverent fear is essential
to our love of God

Catholics as a whole, then, are not in awe of God; they hold themselves to Him by love rather than by fear; yet for all that, there must come into our religion a notion also of fear, else God will be made of little account, dwarfed by His hero-followers, the saints. It is possible that familiarity with God may breed something which seems very like contempt. The majesty of God must be considered just as much as His love, for either without the other would really give a false idea of Him.

Just as there are people who would give up all belief in Hell, because they prefer to concentrate upon His mercy, and, as a result, have no real love of God as He is in Himself, so there are people also who do not sufficiently remember the respect due to His awfulness, people who think of Him as a Redeemer, which indeed He is, but not as a Judge, which is equally His prerogative. Hence this side of our character is also to be made perfect by the indwelling of the Spirit of God: our fear, anger, and hate have got to be sanctified by finding a true object for their due exercise. No single talent must be wrapped away in uselessness; I must fear God, and be angry with and hate sin. Fear, then, as well as piety, is a gift of the Spirit.

The chief way in which the absence of this gift of fear manifests itself is in the careless and slipshod way we perform our duties. We are sure to believe in God's justice and majesty; but we are not so sure to act up to our belief. Accuracy in devotion, in prayer, in life, is the result of a filial fear of God, and if I have to confess a very chaotic and uncertain procedure in my spiritual duties, then I can tell quite easily which gift I most need to make use of.

What are my times of prayer like? Are they as regularly kept to as my circumstances permit? How about my subject for meditation? How about my following of the Mass, my watchfulness in prayer, my days for Confession and Communion? Again, my duties at home, in my profession, in the work I have undertaken: are they, on the whole, punctually performed, accurately, with regard to details? This is where my fear of God should come in, for fear here is part of love, and love is enormously devoted to little things; indeed love finds that where it is concerned, there *are* no little things, but time and place and manner and thoroughness have all got to be noted and carried out faithfully. Here, then, is where I shall find I need a reverential fear of God.

Yes, of course, pride and laziness will protest all the while, by urging that all this is a great deal of fuss about nothing, that God is our Father, that He perfectly understands, that we should not worry ourselves too much over trifles. Now, pride and laziness often speak true things, or rather half-truths. It is true that God is my Father and understands; but it is equally true that I am His child and that love demands my thoroughness. Horror of sin, devotion to the sacrament of Confession, the Scripture saying about a severe judgment for every idle word:[62] all these things have got to be taken into account as well as the first set of principles. Piety needs fear for its perfect performance.

The boy at first may have to be scolded into obedience to his mother. He does not at first realize, and is

[62]Cf. Matt. 12:36.

punished; but watch him when he is a grown man, no longer in subjection or under obedience; see how charmingly he cares for his mother by anticipating her wishes, how much he is at her beck and call, proudly foreseeing for her, protecting, caring. That is love, no doubt, but a love of reverence. They are comrades in a sense, but she is always his mother to him, someone to be idolized, reverenced, and yes, really feared, in the fullest sense of love.

26

Grace is the life of the soul

"The indwelling of the Holy Spirit," then, is a true and magnificent phrase. It means that we become living temples of God. Elsewhere indeed He is in tree, flower, sky, earth, and water; up in the heavens, down to the depths of the lower places in the cleft wood and lifted stone, in the heart of all creation by the very fact of its creation.

Yet the higher a thing is in the scale of being, the more nearly is it in God's image and likeness, so that man, by his sheer intelligence, is more representative of God, as the highest masterpiece is more representative of the author of it. Yet over and above this intelligent life of man is another life in him, which secures God's presence within Him in some nobler fashion, for it is noticeable that Scripture repeatedly speaks of God's dwelling in His saints, and not dwelling in sinners.[63] Now, He is even in sinners by the title of their Creator, so that *dwelling* must be a deliberate phrase chosen by the inspired author of Scripture to represent some presence above the mere general presence of God everywhere.

Consequently we are driven to the conclusion that the saints, in virtue of their sainthood, become dwelling places of God, temples, special places set apart, where in a more perfect way, with richer expression and truer representation, God is. Sanctity, therefore, constitutes something wholly supernatural, attracting God's indwelling, or rather resulting from this indwelling of God.

Now, sanctity itself cannot mean that one man is able to make himself so alluring to God that he draws God to himself, for in that case, God's action of indwelling would be motived by a creature, and God would have found some finite reason for His act. This cannot be, since the only sufficient motive for God can be God Himself. "He hath done all things on account of Himself,"[64] say the Scriptures. We can be sure, therefore,

[63]Cf. Wisd. 1:4.
[64]Cf. Ps. 113b:3 (RSV = Ps. 115:3).

•

that the indwelling of the Spirit is the cause and not the effect of the goodness that is in man, for the saints are not born, but made by God. Hence we understand what is meant by saying that the justice of the saints— their justification—is effected by grace, that is, by God's free gift. It is not from them, but from Him: "Not to us, O Lord, not to us, but to Thy name give glory."[65]

Grace, therefore, is the name given to that divine habit whereby the soul is made one with Him. It is clear, then, also, why in the catechism, grace is called the supernatural life of the soul, and why mortal sin is called the death of the soul, since it kills the soul by depriving it of sanctifying grace.

This leads us to the last notion of grace, that it is in the supernatural order what the soul is in the natural order. My soul is everywhere in my body and gives evidence of its presence by the life there manifest. Cut off a portion of the body, amputate a limb, and it dies; the soul is no longer in it. So does grace work. It is right in the very essence of the soul, at the heart of it, and works through into all the faculties and powers by means of the virtues. It is the life of the whole assemblage of these

[65]Ps. 113b:1 (RSV = Ps. 115:1).

115

habits of goodness. As soon as it is withdrawn, then at once charity goes, for we are out of friendship with God, and charity is nothing other than the love of God. Hope still and faith in some form remain, but without any inner life or energy to quicken them. All else is a crumbled ruin, without shape or life—a sight to fill those who can see it with horror and disgust.

Without grace we are old, worn, dead, not only useless to ourselves, but a pollution to others. Need one wonder if all life is different to the soul in sin? Religion, God, Heaven, Mass, and prayers have lost all attraction and are full of drudgery. Outwardly we feel the same, but our attraction to these higher gifts has gone, a prodigal as yet content with the husks of life's fruitage, relishing only the food of swine, without grace, spiritually dead. With grace the soul is once more thronged with vital activities, for grace is life. It is grace that gives the same charm to the soul as life gives to the body: it imparts a freshness, an alertness, an elasticity, a spontaneous movement, a fragrance, a youth. By grace we are children in God's eyes, with the delicate coloring and sweetness of a child.

Bede Jarrett, O.P. (1881-1934)

Born in England in 1881, Cyril Jarrett received the name Br. Bede when he took the Dominican habit in 1898 at Lancashire. He then studied at Oxford and at Louvain, where he received an additional degree in theology. After his ordination to the priesthood in 1904, he was stationed at St. Dominic's Priory in London. At the age of 33, he was named Prior there and, just two years later, was elected Provincial—an office he would hold for the rest of his life, being re-elected an unprecedented four times.

In addition to attending to his duties as Provincial, which included opening a new church and priory in London, he undertook a demanding schedule of preaching and lecture engagements in England and abroad, and he established an ongoing series of Thomistic lectures in London. Among his scholarly contributions were several historical studies, as well as a lively biography of St. Dominic.

Fr. Jarrett looked upon life as a great adventure, and this joyful spirit pervades and characterizes his writings, which combine a solid foundation in Church doctrine with a down-to-earth insight applicable to everyday living. Reflecting his great understanding of human nature and the mercy and love of God, Fr. Jarrett's works continue to inspire people in all walks of life.

Sophia Institute Press®

Sophia Institute is a nonprofit institution that seeks to restore man's knowledge of eternal truth, including man's knowledge of his own nature, his relation to other persons, and his relation to God.

Sophia Institute Press® serves this end in numerous ways. It publishes translations of foreign works to make them accessible for the first time to English-speaking readers. It brings back into print books that have been long out of print. And it publishes important new books that fulfill the ideals of Sophia Institute. These books afford readers a rich source of the enduring wisdom of mankind.

Sophia Institute Press® makes these high-quality books available to the general public by using advanced technology and by soliciting donations to subsidize its general publishing costs.